中英双语版

企鹅经典 名人大发现

查尔斯·狄更斯

[美]帕姆·波拉克(Pam Pollack)　[美]梅格·贝尔维索(Meg Belviso)◎著
[美]马克·艾德华·盖耶(Mark Edward Geyer)◎绘　潘华凌◎译

Who Was Charles Dickens?

CNS 湖南科学技术出版社 小博集 BOOKY KIDS
·长沙·

著作权合同登记号：字18-2024-193

图书在版编目（CIP）数据

名人大发现. 查尔斯·狄更斯 : 汉英对照 /（美）帕姆·波拉克（Pam Pollack），（美）梅格·贝尔维索（Meg Belviso）著 ; 潘华凌译 ;（美）马克·艾德华·盖耶（Mark Edward Geyer）绘. -- 长沙 : 湖南科学技术出版社，2025. 1. --（企鹅经典）. -- ISBN 978-7-5710-3266-1

Ⅰ. H319. 4

中国国家版本馆CIP数据核字第2024X2K062号

上架建议：科普读物

QI'E JINGDIAN · MINGREN DA FAXIAN：ZHONG-YING SHUANGYU BAN CHA'ERSI DIGENGSI

企鹅经典 · 名人大发现：中英双语版　查尔斯 · 狄更斯

著　　者：［美］帕姆·波拉克（Pam Pollack）　梅格·贝尔维索（Meg Belviso）
绘　　者：［美］马克·艾德华·盖耶（Mark Edward Geyer）
译　　者：潘华凌
出 版 人：潘晓山
责任编辑：刘　竞
策划出品：李　炜　张苗苗　文赛峰
策划编辑：马　瑄
特约编辑：杜佳美
营销编辑：付　佳　杨　朔　周晓茜
装帧设计：利　锐
内文排版：金锋工作室
出　　版：湖南科学技术出版社
（湖南省长沙市芙蓉中路416号　邮编：410008）
网　　址：www.hnstp.com
印　　刷：三河市航远印刷有限公司
经　　销：新华书店
开　　本：875 mm × 1230 mm 1/32
字　　数：107千字
印　　张：5.125
版　　次：2025年1月第1版
印　　次：2025年1月第1次印刷
书　　号：ISBN 978-7-5710-3266-1
定　　价：22.00元

若有质量问题，请致电质量监督电话：010-59096394　　团购电话：010-59320018

目 录

Contents

谁是查尔斯·狄更斯？

沃伦鞋油作坊坐落在伦敦钱多斯街上考文特花园那片繁华市场的西北面。1824 年，这家鞋油作坊的橱窗里呈现了奇特的一幕。过往的男男女女常常被吸引到橱窗前面，驻足观看。

两个男孩并排坐着，一个十二岁，另一个年龄稍大一点。他们的工作就是给鞋油瓶子封口和贴标签。他们每天工作十个小时，每周工作六天。为了完成工作任务，男孩子们必须动作利索。为了增加工作的趣味性，他们玩起了游戏：比一比看谁的动作更快。他们干活的速度可快了，街道上的行人往往会驻足注视他们一番。

那个年龄稍大的男孩是个孤儿，名叫鲍勃·费金。他并不介意人们注视着自己干活。另外那个男孩就是查尔斯·狄更斯。他觉得，坐在沃伦鞋油作坊的橱窗里干活是他能够想象到的最糟糕的事情。

查尔斯梦想着能够上学读书，甚至是像牛津或剑桥那样的英国最好的大学。他热爱阅读，有时甚至自己创作故事。查尔斯的父亲约翰·狄更斯总是入不敷出。约翰深陷债务泥潭后，无力供养自己有七个孩子的家庭。因此，查尔斯只得辍学，被送去做工。他伤心欲绝，窘迫不安。如果他一辈子都被困在鞋油作坊的橱窗里，被街道上的来往行人嘲笑，那该怎么办啊？他怎么都不相信自己的父母会这样对待他。他恳求父母把他“从屈辱和被忽视的境地中解救出来”。

等到查尔斯·狄更斯长大成人后，他创作了许多有关贫穷孩子的小说，他们过着孤独而又艰苦的生活。他的故事后来成为世界上阅读人数最多、最受喜爱的故事之一。

直到查尔斯·狄更斯去世之后，世人才知道，他曾经也是个穷孩子。

第一章

欢迎来到伦敦

1812年2月7日，查尔斯·狄更斯出生在英国的朴次茅斯。他的父亲约翰在海军军需处任职。约翰有稳定的薪水，而且喜欢把钱花费在他自己、朋友们、他妻子以及他的两个孩子范妮和查尔斯身上。在接下来的几年时间里，狄更斯夫妇总共养育着七个孩子。家里有这么多孩子，薪水又有限，约翰本应该在花钱时精打细算。不幸的是，约翰在金钱上从不精打细算。如果他没有钱支付面包的账单，他便会向面包店老板赊欠，以后再付。等到面包店老板上门要求付账时，约翰已经欠了其他许多人的钱——鞋店老板的、肉店老板的和裁缝店老板的。即便到了这个时候，他仍然没有勤俭节约，省下钱来还债，而是到餐馆去吃昂贵的大餐。他总是觉得自己可以在什么地方弄到钱，但他从来都没成功过。

查尔斯五岁时，他家迁居到了查塔姆镇，那是泰晤士河畔的一座军港小镇。查尔斯喜欢待在查塔姆。那儿有许多别的孩子可以和他一起玩耍。他喜欢上学。有时候查尔斯身体不舒服，他的侧腹痛让他必须躺在床上。而家里雇了一个保姆——一个年轻女子，负责照看孩子们。保姆名叫玛丽·韦勒。玛丽给查尔斯讲述神奇的——还有吓人的——睡前故事。他也喜欢自己阅读。他最喜欢阅读的书是《佩里格林·皮克尔》《汤姆·琼斯》和《一千零一夜》。他有时候会自己创作故事，如《印度的苏丹：米斯纳》。他期待将来有一天自己能够成为一个像玛丽那样善于讲故事的人。

查尔斯和他父亲有时候会绕着小镇漫步。一天，他们驻足在盖茨山一幢漂亮的房子前面。房子很大，是砖砌的，可以俯瞰整片乡野。查尔斯说，他很想有朝一日能够住在这幢房子里。他父亲告诉他，如果他非常努力地工作，将来就可以如愿以偿。

1822 年，查尔斯十岁时，他父亲调往英国的首都伦敦。狄更斯一家迁居到了一个名叫卡姆登镇的地方。对查尔斯而言，伦敦是个新世界。当时有一百三十多万人居住在伦敦。这个数字比二十年前多出了二十万。伦敦的人口迅速增长。

由于新的发明不断涌现，工厂工作增加了。曾经居住在乡下的人们现在迁居到了城里，到工厂去工作。那儿的工作往往报酬很低，而且那儿的工作数量满足不了拥向伦敦的所有人的工作需求。父母们外出工作时，许多孩子必须得自己照顾好自己。街道上很脏，也很嘈杂。街道上到处是来往的行人，还有大车、马匹和猪。孩子们饿着肚子，光着脚丫子，身上穿着破烂的衣裤。他们在街道上玩耍和讨钱。上学是一件奢侈的事情，只有有钱的人家才能供得起孩子上学。

在狄更斯位于卡姆登镇的家里，查尔斯睡在主楼梯顶端的一个像衣柜一样的橱柜里。查尔斯的姐姐范妮被

送到了皇家音乐学院去学习唱歌。查尔斯后来再没有上过学，因为家里没有足够的钱供他上学。

查尔斯的母亲制订了各种计划，想要开办一所属于自己的学校。她打发查尔斯出去给新学校做广告宣传，但找上门来的人只有他父亲的那些债主。当债主敲打他们家大门时，他父亲就躲在家里的楼上。约翰·狄更斯有时候会打发查尔斯前往坐落在汉普斯特德路上的当铺。查尔斯会带着餐具、家具甚至他喜爱的书去典当。

全家人挤在两个空房间里，没有钱购买煤炭取暖。他们把家里拥有的一切都拿到当铺去当掉了。

即便在那段艰难困苦的日子里，查尔斯对伦敦的喜爱也还是与日俱增。他喜欢去倾听街道上人们的交谈。他学会了他们的口音和手势，学会了他们使用的方言俚语。只要他听到了一个有关什么人的有趣故事，他就会把这个故事牢牢记下来。

后来，家里的一个朋友想出了一个主意：查尔斯可以到沃伦鞋油作坊去做工挣钱。查尔斯认为，这是个可怕的消息。他感觉到，父母似乎认为他的生命一钱不值。

在鞋油作坊里——刚开始坐落在河岸街三十号，后来搬迁到了钱多斯街——查尔斯与另外两个男孩子鲍勃·费金和波尔·格林一起干活。在短暂的晚餐休息时间，查尔斯需要完成自己的学习。但他的学习持续不了多长时间，因为他像在作坊里干活的其他男孩一样，一周需要工作六天，一天工作十个小时。

鲍勃和波尔有时候管查尔斯叫“小绅士”，因为他的言谈和举止像个受了教育的人。那时候的英国，像鲍勃·费金那样的穷孩子步入“上等”或“上流”社会是非常不同寻常的事情。查尔斯担心，他会一辈子当个作坊的工人，就像鲍勃一样。

童工

随着19世纪工厂和商业的发展，许多孩子被送出去工作。年仅四岁的孩童就已经开始工作了。他们在危险恶劣的条件下每天干活达十六个小时之多。有时候，如果他们被发现干活不够卖力，还会挨打。贫穷的家庭依靠他们的孩子去当学徒、机器操作员、家仆和煤矿工人挣来的钱维持家用。年幼的孩子在工厂里工作，制作像地毯、火柴、钉子之类的东西。每个小时仅有半个便士的劳动报酬。到了20世纪初，人们对残酷的童工现象深恶痛绝。现在，世界上几乎每个国家都制定了禁止使用童工的法律。

查尔斯微薄的薪水不足以替他父亲偿还债务。1824年2月20日，约翰·狄更斯由于无力偿还债务而被关进马夏尔西监狱。

第二章

隐藏着的才华

马夏尔西监狱是一座收监欠债人的监狱。约翰·狄更斯必须得待在里面，直到他还清了债为止。

除了查尔斯和范妮之外，家里其他成员全部住进了马夏尔西监狱。范妮是音乐学院的寄宿生。查尔斯住进了罗伊兰斯太太的公寓里。罗伊兰斯太太专门出租房间给做工的孩子。她没有善待查尔斯。

马夏尔西监狱

坐落在伦敦萨瑟克的马夏尔西监狱于14世纪在泰晤士河畔建成。监狱收监了许多犯下不同罪行的人员，其中包括积欠巨额债务者。有时候，整个家庭都会被收监——而不仅仅是犯了某个罪行的家长。如果被收监者有钱，他们可以在监狱的商店或餐馆购买东西，同时住进条件更好一些的房间。他们还可以出钱购买通行证离开监狱去挣钱偿还债务。许多囚犯在被关押期间会积欠更多债务。而那些最贫穷的人往往挤在条件最简陋的房间里。许多人几个月之内就会饿死。

马夏尔西监狱于19世纪70年代被拆除，现仅存一堵墙，上面有一块标牌，标牌上是查尔斯·狄更斯的一句话：“它现在已经不存在了，而没有了它，世界依然如故。”

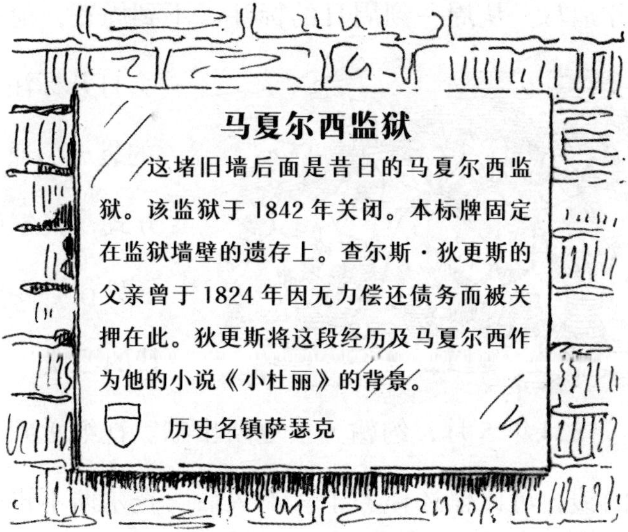

每个周末，查尔斯和范妮都会步行十二英里[①]去看望家人。有一次去监狱看望家人时，查尔斯说服他父亲替他找了个更好的住处，但他对可怕的罗伊兰斯太太一直忘不了。

父亲因欠债惹上牢狱之灾后，查尔斯对债务产生了恐惧。他每周领到薪水后，便会把硬币均匀分成七堆，并把硬币装进一个个小袋子里，在装有硬币的不同袋子上分别写上从周一到周日的标注。不到周三，他绝对不

会打开标注了周三的袋子。通过这种方式，查尔斯养成了只在必要时才花钱的习惯。

1824 年 5 月，约翰 · 狄更斯出狱。他继承到了足够多的钱，可以偿还债务了。不久后，查尔斯不再需要在沃伦鞋油作坊干活了。

---

① 英里：英美制长度单位。1 英里≈1.609 千米。

查尔斯不再工作后，他母亲很生气。她很想把他送回作坊去。查尔斯认为，父亲把他从鞋油作坊解救出来，简直是个英雄，而他的母亲则是个坏人。“事后，我从来都没有忘记，我决不会忘记，我不可能会忘记，我母亲很想把我送回鞋油作坊去。”查尔斯说。家里人后来再没有提起过这件事情。

查尔斯重返学校了。惠灵顿寄宿学校的教师们很严厉，但查尔斯很喜欢那所学校。

在鞋油作坊干了许多个月活之后，他尽情投身到游戏、戏剧和笑话之中。他把老鼠和蜜蜂藏匿在课桌抽屉里，制作微型驿站马车，让老鼠坐在上面。

他创作故事并编辑、印制自己的报纸。其他同学用弹珠来换报纸。他假装说着自己捏造出来的外国话，惹得同学们哈哈大笑。

仅仅两年过后，查尔斯十五岁时，他父亲再次陷入债务泥潭，无力再支付他上学的费用。1827 年 5 月，查尔斯到埃利斯和布莱克莫尔律师事务所担任初级文员。

上班第一天，他戴了一顶在颌下系带子的军帽。他的几个新雇主派他外出办差，返回时他却被人打得眼睛都肿了！

查尔斯解释说，街上有个人取笑他头上戴的帽子，并且把他的帽子拍掉了。于是，他们打了起来。雇主们没有因为事情的经过感到震惊，但他们因为他叙述故事的方式感到震惊。他把事情的经过表演给他们看，扮演双方的角色，还加上了一些旁观者的角色。他模仿那人

取笑他的帽子时，他的雇主们忍不住哈哈笑起来。

埃利斯和布莱克莫尔与他们的年轻文员说话越多，就越惊讶于他对伦敦的了解程度——他熟悉伦敦的街道，熟悉伦敦的典故，熟悉伦敦丰富多彩的人物。他们新来的文员身上隐藏着讲述故事的才华！

第三章

让读者认识博兹

查尔斯在律师事务所担任文员至1829年。他十七岁时成了法院的一个报纸记者。他有时候会创作滑稽的故事，指出当时法律的不公正现象。对查尔斯而言，法院是观察人们的表现和听有趣故事的另一个地方。

这期间，查尔斯遇见了一个名叫玛丽亚·比得奈尔的姑娘。她是一个银行家的女儿。查尔斯疯狂地爱上了她。有些夜晚，他在凌晨两点离开法院后步行数英里，站在她家住宅的前面。他给她的父母写信，说尽管他没有很多钱，但他和他们的女儿是很般配的一对。

玛丽亚的家人并不为之所动。她母亲甚至都懒得去弄明白查尔斯的姓名。她管他叫“狄金先生”。1832 年，玛丽亚的父母送她出国前往巴黎了。

随着玛丽亚的离开，查尔斯集中精力到了写作上。1833 年年底，查尔斯创作了一篇有关一对表兄弟用晚餐的滑稽短篇故事。他将这篇题为《白杨园的晚餐》的短篇故事投入“舰队街上一幢昏暗的公寓大楼的一间昏暗办公室的一个昏暗信箱”里。这便是《月刊》杂志的编辑部。数天过后，查尔斯购买了那本杂志，发现上面登载了那篇故事！

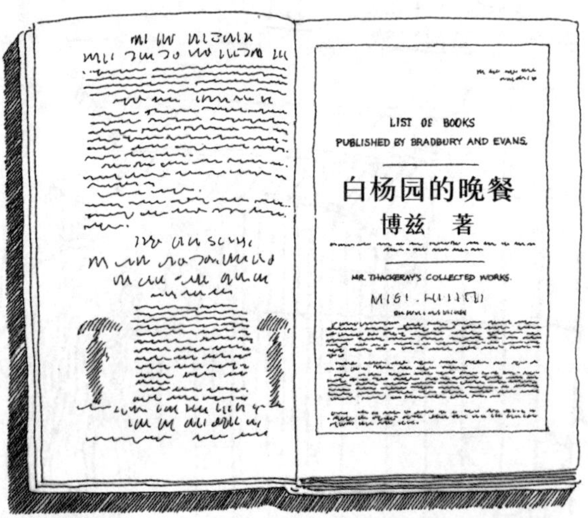

这篇短篇故事并没有署上查尔斯的名字。他甚至没有收到作品的稿酬，但《月刊》杂志想要这个年轻作者更多的作品。他没有在杂志上署“查尔斯·狄更斯”这个名字，而是署了“博兹”一名。他借用了他最小弟弟奥古斯塔斯的名字。家里人给他弟弟取了“摩西”这个绰号。奥古斯塔斯还是个蹒跚学步的孩童，他将这个绰号念成“博西斯”，“博兹”就是这个发音的简称。

查尔斯想要创作一部篇幅更长的小说，关于一群组建一个俱乐部的朋友的故事。他的第一部小说《匹克威克外传》刚开始没有以书的形式出版，而是从1836年3月开始，每月登载一章。人们喜爱查尔斯笔下的人物，特别是仆人萨姆·韦勒。查尔斯描写的韦勒说话带着

萨姆·韦勒

伦敦的腔调，他听到伦敦街道上的人们就是那样说话的：“给你带来个人的不便，非常对不住，夫人。入室盗窃者把老夫人放在火上烤时，对她这么说……”

所有人都在谈论《匹克威克外传》和博兹。谁都不知道查尔斯·狄更斯才是小说的真正作者。但这种情况很快就会改变。

小说连载

在19世纪，许多小说都是一段时间写一章。每月在杂志上发表一个章节。一本杂志通常为三十二页，用绿纸包装。读者会购买该杂志的每一期，以便阅读小说接下来的部分。这种方式对出版商很有利，因为可以促使读者热衷于购买杂志。对手头不宽裕的人而言，一个月花费几个便士就可以读到一本小说，是可以承受的。

整部小说一旦完成，出版商就会出售装订成册的书籍。那些出得起钱的读者就会购买整部完整的小说。

查尔斯·狄更斯与不止一家出版商签订了出版合同。每份合同都协定，查尔斯将替该出版商分期创作完成一部小说。他的第一部小说《匹克威克外传》是由查普曼－霍尔出版社出版的。他同一时期创作的《雾都孤儿》在《本特利文集》上连载，然后由理查德·本特利出版社出版。

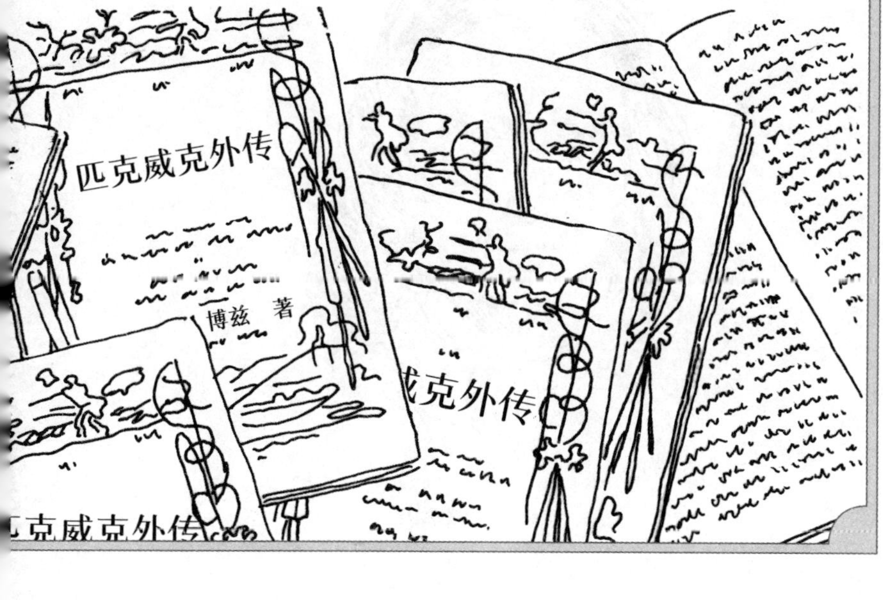

查尔斯取得了成功，于是觉得是时候娶妻成家了。他没有再遇见像玛丽亚·比得奈尔那样值得爱的女人，而1836年年初，一个报纸编辑为他介绍认识了自己的女儿凯瑟琳·霍格思。即便查尔斯并非在严格意义上爱凯瑟琳，但他也是十分喜欢她。他与她妹妹玛丽是非常要好的朋友。1836年4月2日，凯瑟琳与查尔斯结婚。一个月之后，他们开始等待他们的第一个孩子降生。

凯瑟琳·霍格思

第四章

一个崭新的世界

查尔斯和凯瑟琳带着凯瑟琳的妹妹玛丽迁居到了伦敦的霍尔本区。

查尔斯虽然尚未完成《匹克威克外传》的写作，但他还是签了一份合同，开始创作一部新小说。《雾都孤儿》讲述的是一个孤儿的故事。这个孤儿因要求更多食物

奥利弗·特威斯特乞讨食物

而被赶出济贫院。他逃到了伦敦，误入了一个贼窝。那群盗贼领头的是奸诈狡猾的道奇和无恶不作的费金。后者的名字源于查尔斯在沃伦鞋油作坊干活时的老朋友。

查尔斯同时创作两部小说，用鹅毛笔奋笔疾书。他每个月都要替两部小说各写一章。两部小说差异非常大。《匹克威克外传》的主人公享受有趣的奇遇时，奥利弗·特威斯特则在逃跑求生。

除了给《月刊》杂志写稿之外，查尔斯还辞去了法

济贫院

济贫院是英国的穷人可以干活换吃住的地方。由于住在济贫院的人不掌握什么技能，他们往往要干艰苦乏味的工作，诸如打碎石块和解开旧绳子以便其中的纤维能够被再次利用。济贫院

里的生活很不舒服，但总还是比流落街头要好一些。济贫院里的儿童可以享受一定的教育和医疗服务，而这些东西他们在济贫院之外是享受不到的。直到 1948 年，《国民救助法》通过之后，英国最后一座济贫院才被关闭。

院报道的工作，担任了《本特利文集》的编辑。他挑选故事，确认那些篇章被准确地刊印出来，并帮助其他作者。绝大多数人都会认为这些工作——创作一部小说、创作第二部小说或编辑《本特利文集》——中的任何一项都是全职工作，需要付出全部的时间才能完成。但是查尔斯同时做了这三件事，还在创作一部剧本！

1837 年 1 月，查尔斯的儿子查利出生了。查尔斯称他的新生儿子为“婴儿现象”。查利仅仅出生几周之后，查尔斯写下了奥利弗·特威斯特出生的场景，或许他从自己的儿子身上获得了灵感。

狄更斯的家庭生活幸福快乐。可是，1837 年 5 月 7 日，查尔斯听见小姨子玛丽的卧室里传来一声尖叫。她病得很严重，几分钟前她还是好好的。她当时才十七岁。然而，翌日下午，玛丽在查尔斯的怀里去世。负责诊治的医生们认为，她可能是心脏出了问题。

那一个月，《匹克威克外传》和《雾都孤儿》没有新的章节问世。查尔斯悲痛欲绝，无法写作。他在创作生

涯中唯有这次没有按时交稿。

玛丽去世后，查尔斯和凯瑟琳离开伦敦度假。查尔斯与一个担任文学编辑的新朋友约翰·福斯特一起待了很长时间。他们之间从此缔结了终生的友谊。

约翰·福斯特

查尔斯随后创作的小说包括以他的真实姓名出版的《尼古拉斯·尼可贝》和《巴纳比·拉奇》。他的小说《老古玩店》在美国风靡一时，因此，当登载该小说新一章的杂志抵达，人们都会站在码头上大声呐喊，询问有关年轻的女主人公的消息："小内尔还活着吗？"查尔斯曾多次认真地考虑访问美国。他常常收到美国小说迷的信件。

1842 年 1 月 2 日，查尔斯和凯瑟琳乘船前往美国。他们把孩子们——儿子查利及两个女儿玛米和凯蒂——留在英国。

美国有很多事情是查尔斯不喜欢的。美国的出版商

们不支付他报酬便拿他的作品去挣钱！查尔斯抱怨时，记者就会发表对他不太友好的报道。他所到之处，都有成群的美国书迷跟随着他。报纸上说，查尔斯“灵气多于优雅，智慧多于美貌”。查尔斯习惯做描述他人的人，

不习惯阅读有关他自己的描述！

1842 年 6 月 29 日，查尔斯和凯瑟琳返回英国。凯瑟琳的另一个妹妹乔治娜过来与他们一起生活。查尔斯很高兴能离开美国，他将美国描述为一个“被一伙流氓驱动”的国家。

第五章

斯克鲁奇和米考伯

1843 年 12 月，查尔斯完成了一部小说，讲述三个鬼魂在圣诞之夜造访一个吝啬老人的故事。

雅各布 · 马利警告三个鬼魂

《圣诞颂歌》以小开本出版，红色布纹封面，书页有烫金饰边。仅仅五天时间便出售了六千册！

《圣诞颂歌》轰动一时。

1 月份，狄更斯夫妇迎来了另一个儿子弗朗西斯。查尔斯和凯瑟琳现在已经有五个子女了。

查尔斯的女儿玛米曾说，她父亲伏案激情写作，然后跳起来走到镜子前面。他做着各种各样的鬼脸，然后又跑回去继续写作。他三番五次返回镜子前面，表演各种场面，大声说话。他甚至都没有看见在场的玛米。他完全变成了自己努力刻画的人物。

那些人物最终给查尔斯带来了他从小渴望的保障。查尔斯现在有钱了。他想要用钱来帮助他人。

《圣诞颂歌》

《圣诞颂歌》不仅改变了人们对查尔斯·狄更斯的看法，还改变了人们对圣诞节的看法。有些历史学家相信，英国的许多节假日传统习惯——诸如社交聚会、家庭团聚、圣诞宴会、舞会和游戏等——均受了这部小说的启示。“斯克鲁奇”这个名字后来泛指吝啬和不厚道的人，恰如“呸，哼！”变成“胡说八道！”之意一样。连“圣诞快乐”这个短语都因为这部小说而家喻户晓。《圣诞颂歌》出版几个月后，英国的慈善捐款数额激增。人们受到感染，表现得很是慷慨！美国的一个工厂主被故事深深感动了，他让自己工厂的所有工人圣诞节休假，还给他们每人一只火鸡！

除了约翰·福斯特，查尔斯的新朋友中没有任何一个人熟悉他的家庭背景。约翰是查尔斯唯一对其讲述过自己家世背景的人。但 1849 年，查尔斯开始创作《大卫·科波菲尔》。这部小说中的许多细节来自他自己真实的生活——查尔斯的父亲喜欢挥霍、收监欠债人的监狱、辍学去鞋油作坊工作、他小气的房东太太。他让这些情节变成了一部畅销书。许多人都阅读过《大卫·科波菲尔》，以至于这部小说开始影响人们的说话方式。如果某个人总是债务缠身但却乐呵呵地指望着可以从什么地方弄到钱。根据小说中的一个人物，此人便会被称为“米考伯”。

大卫·科波菲尔和他的朋友米考伯

乌拉尼亚居所

1846 年 5 月，查尔斯与一个名叫安杰拉·伯德特－库茨的女继承人一起为无家可归的妇女建立了一个家。查尔斯不想让妇女因为她们面临的问题而受到责备。他想要给她们提供教育和家政技能培训。他想要给予她们希望。

1847 年至 1859 年间，超过一百个妇女从乌拉尼亚居所毕业。

查尔斯的朋友们都知道“米考伯”就是约翰·狄更斯，但他们仍然没有想到，他曾进过收监欠债人的监狱。

当年的年底，已经离开了《本特利文集》编辑岗位若干年的查尔斯决定创立他自己的月刊《家常话》。刊物上登载查尔斯本人和他的朋友威廉·撒克里以及威尔基·科林斯的小说。

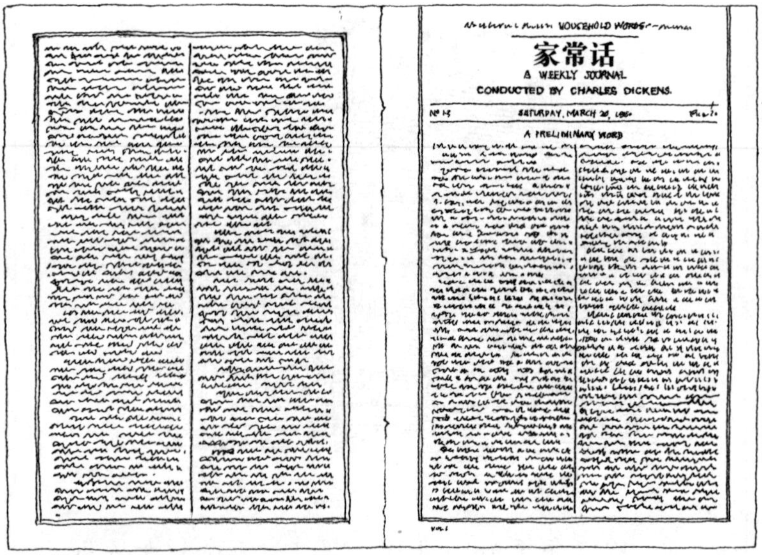

1850 年 8 月，凯瑟琳生下了第九个孩子多拉·安妮·狄更斯。凯瑟琳如此频繁地怀孕真的很不容易。她

威尔基·科林斯（1824—1889）

威尔基·科林斯是小说家、剧作家和查尔斯·狄更斯的挚友。他最著名的小说包括《白衣女人》和第一部英语侦探小说《月亮宝石》。《月亮宝石》是他最受欢迎的小说，而且为其他侦探小说诸如《福尔摩斯探案集》奠定了基础。他谈及自己早年与狄更斯的交往情况时说：“我们每天都会见面，而且彼此之间的欣赏到了极致。”

的妹妹乔治娜常常负责照看孩子们。凯瑟琳不经常见到查尔斯，因为他总是忙于工作。她甚至都无法与他正常散步，因为他走路的速度太快了。他说他的灵感来自人

来人往的街道。他有时候一走就是三十英里！凯瑟琳越是感到疲惫，查尔斯似乎就越精力旺盛。

1851年，多拉还在襁褓中，约翰·狄更斯因胆囊手术引起的并发症去世。不管父亲给自己带来了多少麻烦，查尔斯都原谅了他，并且偿还了他的一切债务。

父亲去世两周之后，襁褓中的多拉夭折了。查尔斯伤心欲绝，但他一如既往地不停工作。

第六章

重返盖茨山

查尔斯忙于写《荒凉山庄》，编辑《家常话》月刊，以及管理乌拉尼亚居所，极少有时间放松自己。他患上肾炎后，仅仅停止工作了六天。

1852 年，凯瑟琳生下了她的第十个也是最后一个孩子爱德华。查尔斯开始在给朋友的信中提及家庭矛盾。他与凯瑟琳之间越来越疏远了，但查尔斯从未说明缘由。在查尔斯的下一部小说《艰难时世》中，主人公娶了一个并不适合他的女人为妻，但法律不允许他与妻子离婚。许多人认为，这样的描述反映了狄更斯自己的婚姻。

查利·狄更斯已经十八岁了，在伊顿公学上学。查尔斯计划将自己的二儿子沃尔特送到印度去替一家英国公司做事。外人看来，查尔斯的家庭似乎很完美——恰如他在自己主编的杂志上编写的那些小说中刻画的家庭一样。

沃尔特·狄更斯和查利·狄更斯

1855年2月，查尔斯访问查塔姆时看到，他以前非常喜欢的位于盖茨山的那幢房子正在出售，于是决定把它买下来。他勤奋工作了许多年，现在终于可以住进自己曾经非常喜爱的房子里面了。

同年 11 月，查尔斯和威尔基·科林斯共同创作了一部名为《冰冻之海》的戏剧。剧本以富兰克林探险队为原型创作，一群英国探险家于十年前，也就是 1845 年，

在北极地区失踪。人们近期发现了他们冻着的遗体。

剧本描述了探险家们最后数日的情景。查尔斯扮演探险队队长理查德·沃杜尔这个主角。他还是剧作的导演兼舞台监督。

《冰冻之海》在英国获得了巨大成功。人们喜爱查尔斯对必死无疑的理查德·沃杜尔的表演。查尔斯的小姨子乔治娜扮演了剧中的角色，他的女儿玛米和凯蒂同样扮演了剧中的角色。他们甚至为维多利亚女王进行了私下的演出。

1857 年 8 月，十六岁的沃尔特·狄更斯离开英国前往印度后不久，查尔斯应邀到自由贸易大厅演出《冰冻

之海》。那是一座大型剧场。查尔斯到那个大舞台表演需要专业女演员。一个朋友推荐了弗朗西丝·特南和她的三个女儿范妮、玛丽亚和埃伦（即人们常说的内莉）。

维多利亚女王（1819—1901）

维多利亚女王从1837年6月到她去世一直担任大不列颠及爱尔兰联合王国的君主。她维护了自己国家的和平安宁和繁荣昌盛。在她担任君主期间，包括科学、工业、工程、娱乐以及医学在内的许多领域都有令人振奋的新发现。

她担任君主的时期非常重要，因此，19世纪在英国被称为“维多利亚时代”。这段时期内有许多伟大的小说问世，其中包括《爱丽丝漫游仙境》《简·爱》以及《福尔摩斯探案集》。

第七章

最糟糕的时代

内莉·特南

内莉·特南遇见查尔斯时年仅十八岁。查尔斯的朋友们都知道，查尔斯深深地爱着她，但查尔斯在公开场合说，他们只是朋友。凯瑟琳从未说过查尔斯的坏话。她满足了他的愿望，他们现在基本分居。

到了1858年，查尔斯与孩子们和他们的姨妈乔治娜住在盖茨山。凯瑟琳与一个女管家住在伦敦。由于当时法律的缘故，离婚非常昂贵，几乎没有什么人能够如愿离婚。于是，他们同意分开生活。

查尔斯的生活比以往任何时候都忙碌。有个朋友去世后，查尔斯想要替他的家庭募集钱款。他创作了新版的《圣诞颂歌》，并向公众朗诵。他运用不同的声音，表演了全部角色。他的表演受到了观众的喜爱。查尔斯也

很喜爱此类表演——也喜欢表演挣到的钱。他在英格兰、苏格兰和爱尔兰进行了为期三个月的巡回演出，朗诵自己的作品。

人们对狄更斯夫妇的婚姻有诸多闲言碎语。查尔斯对此怒不可遏。

如果查尔斯的朋友们支持凯瑟琳，他就会与他们绝交！他甚至为此与《家常话》的其他员工大打出手。1859年1月，他宣布杂志停刊。他甚至停止了对乌拉尼亚居所的管理工作。

面对查尔斯的所作所为，朋友们惊愕不已，他的子女们也是如此。他现在声称，孩子们根本不爱凯瑟琳，凯瑟琳也根本不爱他们。当子女们跟他们的母亲说话时，他就会生他们的气。他女儿凯蒂后来说，父亲的行为“像个疯子”。

盖茨山的住宅已经变成了一处令人悲伤的可怕之所。1860年7月，凯蒂嫁给了威尔基·科林斯多病的画家弟弟查尔斯，从而摆脱了家庭。凯蒂的婚礼当天，玛米发

现自己的父亲抓着凯蒂的婚纱哭了。他责备自己迫使她离开家庭。凯瑟琳甚至都没有受邀去参加婚礼。

查尔斯把精力投入到了他创办的新杂志《一年四季》

上。查尔斯决定在该刊上连载他的下一部小说。小说讲述的是法国大革命。查尔斯经历了一段艰难的时期才开始创作这部小说。最后,《双城记》开场白成了有史以来的小说中最著名的开场白:“这是最好的时代,也是最坏的时代。”

第八章

新的旅程

盖茨山居住区有一处墓地。有个家庭竖了十三块墓碑，标示十三个夭折的孩子。这让查尔斯萌生了创作《远大前程》的想法。小说将在《一年四季》上继《双城记》之后连载。小说开篇描写了一座教堂的墓地。贫穷的孤儿皮普在那儿遇见了一个逃犯。多年之后，皮普有了机会，可以成为一位绅士并且进入上流社会。

小皮普

《远大前程》问世之后，查尔斯继续他的朗诵之旅。由于与许多亲友关系破裂，众叛亲离，他只能从因他的作品而喜爱他的读者那儿获得巨大的安慰。1863 年 9 月，母亲离世，但查尔斯没有像当初原谅父亲那样原谅她。对母亲曾经想要他返回沃伦鞋油作坊干活这事，他一直耿耿于怀。几个月之后，即 1863 年 12 月，查尔斯的儿子沃尔特在印度去世。

1865年6月，查尔斯、内莉和内莉的母亲搭乘火车前往伦敦。

火车在通过肯特郡的一座桥梁时脱轨了。火车断成两段。查尔斯和特南母女被甩到了半悬在桥上的一节车

厢的一个角落里。查尔斯后来向一个朋友描述了当时的情景：“火车的车厢被毁坏了，超重的东西压在人们身上，他们歪着身子处在铁器和木料中间，满身是泥，衣服湿透了，现场一片混乱。那种场景简直无法想象。”

查尔斯从窗口爬出去，把内莉母女带到了等待着的救护列车上。他返回去帮助那些在脱轨事故中受困的人。他坐在受伤和奄奄一息的乘客身边。然后，他爬回他自己的车厢去取回他正在创作的小说书稿：《我们共同的朋友》。

随后一年，查尔斯制订了一个前往美国的特别计划。

1867 年，查尔斯再次赴美。这次的美国之行比 1842 年的第一次访问更加理想。民众喜爱他的朗诵。他面见了老朋友们。他没有面对自己小说的销售问题，而是为欢迎他和替他笔下的人物喝彩的书迷表演。

查尔斯的身体并非处于最佳状态。他的一只脚有时候会肿胀，以至于无法走路。他吃东西也很困难。然而，他还是一路前行，从波士顿到纽约，再到费城，再到华盛顿特区。安德鲁·约翰逊总统甚至参加了他的一次朗诵会，并且邀请他到白宫做客。

查尔斯毫不后悔重返美国。他于 1868 年 5 月乘船回国。他在船上便计划再来一次朗诵之旅。

凯特·威金（1856—1923）

在一列从缅因州开往波士顿的火车上，一个来自费城的十二岁女孩悄悄溜到了大文豪查尔斯·狄更斯旁边的座位上。她把他的所有小说都阅读了好几遍，不过，“当然，（她确实）时不时会略过某些非常枯燥的部分。她略过的不是那些简短的枯燥部分，而是那些冗长的。”他们谈论着哪些部分是枯燥的，哪些作品是他们最喜欢的——他们两个人都最喜欢《大卫·科波菲尔》。凯特·威金从未忘记那次与她最喜爱的作家同行的旅程，即便在她长大成了畅销书作家后也还是如此。

1903年，凯特·威金出版了《森尼布鲁克农场的丽贝卡》。

第九章

惊恐到最后

美国之行后，有些人可能期待查尔斯·狄更斯会在1868年夏季好好休息。而他却计划了一次新的秘密的表演，此举令他的朋友们深感惊讶。

那年夏末，他儿子亨利离家前往剑桥大学三一学院攻读数学。爱德华准备去澳大利亚他哥哥阿尔弗雷德那里一起务农。

查尔斯于当年10月开始了他的朗诵之旅。11月，查利成了《一年四季》的编辑。

同月，查尔斯

公布了他正在计划的表演项目。《雾都孤儿》中，一个名叫比尔·赛克斯的罪犯发现他的女友南希企图帮助孤儿奥利弗。盛怒之下，他杀了女友。他对自己做的事情感到惶恐不安，逃跑了，后来被警察消灭了。查尔斯准备把故事情景全部搬上舞台。

那场面惊心动魄。查尔斯扮演邪恶的比尔·赛克斯一角，让自己进入了一种狂热的状态，令观众感到太过真实。查尔斯在自己的场景剧本上给自己写下了一条批注：“惊恐到最后。”这也正是他给观众带来的感受。

表演结束后，他精疲力竭，得有人搀扶着他下台。但他一旦感受好些了，便又想再次表演。像任何伟大的演员一样，他喜爱那种对观众的影响力。

查尔斯的医生嘱咐他要完全退出巡演，但他拒绝了。医生叮嘱查利·狄更斯每场表演都要到场。如果他父亲似乎要倒下了——医生叮嘱他："你必须跑上舞台，

抓住他……要不然，天啊，他会直接死在所有人面前的！”1869年4月，查尔斯暂停了巡演，但他不愿意完全停下来。

休息期间，查尔斯与查普曼–霍尔出版社签订了一份合同，创作一部由十二部分组成的新小说：《艾德温·德鲁德之谜》。

查尔斯希望聘请他的女婿查尔斯·科林斯为这部新小说画插图。凯蒂的丈夫需要钱，但他身体过于虚弱，无法承担这项工作。凯蒂嫁给了一个身体不健康的丈夫，查尔斯一直都不舒心。他后来说，查尔斯·科林斯真的会“在整个自然生命期间随时因健康原因倒下”。像查尔斯·狄更斯这样充满活力的人，查尔斯·科林斯对他来说一定很难理解。

查尔斯的一只脚仍然很痛，一只手臂麻木。他可能中风了，但他对此置之不理。1869 年圣诞节的大部分时间里，他都在盖茨山楼上，无法下楼。一天晚上，他来到一些家人身边玩传统的客厅游戏。他们在进行一个记忆游戏时，每个人都必须背诵一份物品清单，并且为下一个人增加一件物品。他们的游戏持续了一段时间后，

他儿子亨利说："查尔斯成功地背诵了一长串单词，并在最后以他自己的经历结束：'沃伦鞋油作坊，斯特兰德街三十号！'"

狄更斯的子女

凯瑟琳和查尔斯的全部子女都由父亲取了特别的绰号。他们经历了很不相同的人生：

查尔斯——查利——成了《一年四季》杂志的编辑。

玛米——柔和的光泽——终生未婚，在查尔斯去世后与姨妈乔治娜一起生活。

凯蒂——金星盒——成了寡妇，然后嫁给了一个画家，她本人也成了画家。

沃尔特——年轻的头骨——在印度英年早逝。

弗朗西斯——追鸡者——在加拿大加入了皇家骑警。

阿尔弗雷德——桑普森黄铜或撞柱游戏——成了澳大利亚的农场主。

悉尼——海洋幽灵或海军上将——成了皇家海军军官。

亨利——H 先生——成了备受尊敬的法官。

爱德华——普罗尼什门特或普罗恩——进入了澳大利亚政界。

查尔斯说这句话时，眼睛里透出怪异的光，仿佛觉得那些词对他有特殊的含义。亨利不知道那是什么含义。时间过去了将近五十年，查尔斯仍然对自己在鞋油作坊干活带来的羞辱感耿耿于怀，仍然对几乎所有人三缄其口。

第十章

诗人角

查尔斯·狄更斯不再是沃伦鞋油作坊橱窗里的那个男孩。他是世界上最出名的作家。他创作的小说超过十五部。他游遍欧洲和北美。他被崇拜他的读者追捧。他出现在剧场前面，身边围满了他的小说迷。他的作品被翻译成了许多语言。连他最不出名的小说都很畅销。他收到了世界各地读者的来信。他创造的词语被收入了词典。他全家人曾经面临被逐出家门的威胁，现在他拥有了不止一幢美丽住宅，包括他小时候梦寐以求的那幢。令人惊叹的是，他广受读者欢迎达数十年之久。

1870 年 3 月 31 日，《艾德温 · 德鲁德之谜》第一章与读者见面。杂志出版后头几天就销售了令人吃惊的五万本。《匹克威克外传》出版三十四年之后，查尔斯 · 狄更斯再次轰动一时。“他曾让父辈感到开心，现在又让子辈感到开心。”伦敦的《泰晤士报》这样评价他。

查尔斯住在盖茨山时，每天上午都会在一座瑞士风格的小木屋里写作。小木屋是一个朋友送给他的，从瑞士寄来散件再拼装。查尔斯喜欢在小木屋的楼上写作，四周墙壁上的镜子映照出室外的那片树林和那条河流。

1870 年 6 月 4 日，凯蒂前来看望父亲。他们进行了一次长谈。凯蒂听见父亲说的话后感到很惊讶。父亲对

女儿说，他懊悔自己没能够成为更加理想的父亲和更加优秀的男人。他谈到了自己与内莉的关系和自己婚姻的结局。凯蒂后来说，他当时说话的情形“仿佛他的生命要结束了，一切都烟消云散了”。

凯蒂次日离开了。6 月 8 日，查尔斯在那幢小木屋里写作，度过了上午。查尔斯很少在下午工作，但当天午饭后，他返回小木屋完成《艾德温·德鲁德之谜》第六章的写作。

当晚与小姨子乔治娜一起吃饭时，查尔斯中风了。凯蒂和玛米急忙赶回家探视。第二天，他在睡梦中去世了。当天是 1870 年 6 月 9 日。查尔斯·狄更斯享年仅五十八岁。

查尔斯原本计划让人把他葬在罗切斯特大教堂墓地，但他的国家执意要把他葬在威斯敏斯特教堂墓地。威斯敏斯特教堂是英国最著名的教堂。英国历史上众多伟大的作家都葬在那里的诗人角。查尔斯去世后，伦敦《泰晤士报》发表社论：查尔斯应该被葬在诗人角。威斯敏斯特教堂的院长同意把他葬在那里。这是个莫大的荣耀——查尔斯的家人不可能拒绝这种荣耀。

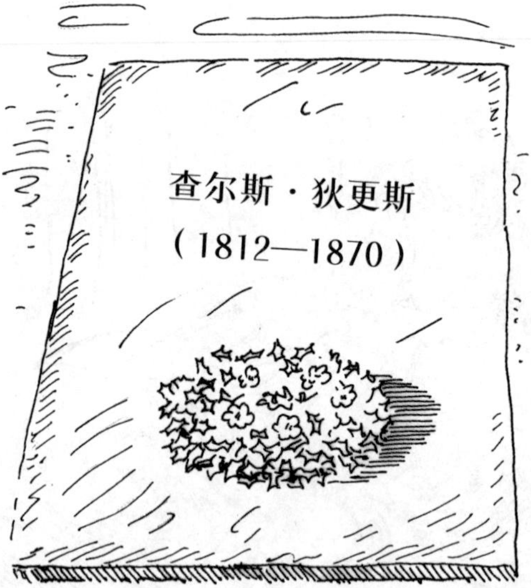

查尔斯成了英国最伟大的作家之一。他下葬时，世人为他举行了一个小型的私人葬礼，前来献花的人太多了，教堂只得开放墓地，持续两天，供民众前来悼念。各行各业的人们来到威斯敏斯特教堂，向他告别。

英国没有其他人像他一样受到各个阶层人们的爱戴，受到富人和穷人的爱戴。直到今天，每年他的生日，人们都会到他的墓地摆放一个花圈。人们第一次知道，查尔斯并没有享受读者们认为的那种幸福快乐的童年。人们知道了，大卫·科波菲尔在很大程度上就是查

尔斯·狄更斯本人。他们明白了，查尔斯对社会各个阶层的人们都充满了同情，因为他曾经贫穷过，也富有过。正是他一直隐瞒的那段人生经历——身处贫穷的环境，做着艰苦的事情，承受监狱带来的羞耻——使他的作品别具一格，受到众多读者的喜爱。

查尔斯·狄更斯生平年表

1812 年 — 查尔斯·狄更斯在朴次茅斯出生。

1817 年 — 狄更斯一家迁居英国的查塔姆镇。

1822 年 — 狄更斯一家迁居英国的伦敦。

1824 年 — 查尔斯开始在沃伦鞋油作坊做事。

1825 年 — 查尔斯重返学校。

1833 年 — 短篇小说《白杨园的晚餐》在《月刊》杂志发表。

1836 年 — 查尔斯娶凯瑟琳·霍格思为妻。

1837 年 — 凯瑟琳的妹妹玛丽·霍格思去世。

1842 年 — 查尔斯访问美国。

1843 年 —《圣诞颂歌》出版。

1846 年 — 乌拉尼亚居所建立。

1850 年 —《家常话》第一期出版发行。

1854 年 —《艰难时世》出版。

1857 年 — 查尔斯与妻子分居。

1859 年 —《双城记》出版。

1865 年 — 查尔斯在肯特郡遭遇火车脱轨事故。

1867 年 — 查尔斯再次访问美国。

1870 年 — 查尔斯去世。

世界大事记

约 970 年 —— 威斯敏斯特教堂动工兴建。
1450 年 —— 德国谷登堡印社创立。
1606 年 —— 威廉·莎士比亚创作《麦克白》。
1666 年 —— 伦敦大火摧毁了大半座城市。
1749 年 —— 亨利·菲尔丁的《汤姆·琼斯》出版。
1770 年 —— 路德维希·凡·贝多芬出生。
1789 年 —— 法国大革命爆发。
1795 年 —— 拿破仑·波拿巴入侵荷兰。
1812 年 —— 1812 年战争爆发。
1825 年 —— 日本向外国船只关闭诸港口。
1830 年 —— 波兰反抗俄国的统治。
1837 年 —— 维多利亚即位，成为英国女王。
1852 年 —— 魔鬼岛罪犯流放地开始设立。
1857 年 —— 美国好莱坞电影基地创立。
1865 年 —— 第一台用于商业销售的打字机诞生。

Who Was Charles Dickens?

On Chandos Street in London, just northwest of Covent Garden's bustling markets, Warren's factory produced blacking paste, which was used for shoe polish. In 1824, there was a curious show in the window of Warren's blacking factory. Ladies and gentleman were often drawn to the window to see it.

Two boys, one twelve years old, the other a little older, sat side by side. Their job was to seal and label the blacking jars. They worked six days a week for ten hours a day. The boys had to be quick to get their work done. To make the day interesting they'd made a game of it, competing to see who could be fastest.They were so speedy that people on the street stopped to stare at them.

The older boy was an orphan named Bob Fagin. He

didn't mind people watching him work. The other boy was Charles Dickens. For him, sitting in the window of Warren's blacking factory was the worst thing he could imagine.

Charles dreamed of going to school, maybe even one of the great English universities like Oxford or Cambridge. He loved to read and sometimes even wrote stories of his own. John Dickens, Charles's father, always spent more money than he earned. When John fell into debt, he could no longer afford his family of seven children. So Charles was taken out of school and sent to work. He was heartbroken and embarrassed. What if he spent his whole life trapped in a factory window, laughed at by people on the street? He couldn't believe his parents had done this to him. He prayed to be "lifted out of the humiliation and neglect."

When Charles grew up, he would write many stories about poor children living lonely, harsh lives. His stories would become some of the most widely read and beloved books in the world.

It wasn't until after his death that people learned Charles Dickens was once one of those poor children, too.

Chapter 1

Welcome to London

Charles Dickens was born in Portsmouth, England, on February 7, 1812. His father, John, worked for the Navy Pay Office. John earned a steady salary and he liked to spend money on himself, his friends, his wife, and his two children, Fanny and Charles. Over the next few years, the Dickenses would have seven children in all. With so many children, and a limited salary, John needed to be very careful about how he spent his money. Unfortunately, John was never careful about money. If he didn't have money to pay for bread, he would put it on a bill at the baker's to pay later. By the time the baker was demanding to be paid, John owed money to many other people—the shoemaker, the butcher, the tailor.

Even then, instead of saving every penny to pay them back, he would have an expensive meal at a restaurant. He always just imagined he'd find the money somewhere, but he never did.

When Charles was five, his family moved to Chatham, a naval town on the Thames River. Charles loved Chatham. He had lots of other children to play with. He enjoyed school. Sometimes Charles did not feel well. He suffered with pains in his side that kept him in bed. But his family had a nursemaid—a young woman who looked after the children. She was named Mary Weller. Mary told wonderful—and terrifying—bedtime stories to Charles.He also loved to read on his own. His favorite books were *Peregrine Pickle*, *Tom Jones*, and *Tales of the Arabian Nights*. Sometimes he wrote stories of his own, like "Misnar, Sultan of India." He hoped one day to become as good a storyteller as Mary.

Sometimes Charles and his father took walks around the town. One day they stopped in front of a beautiful house on Gad's Hill. It was large and made of brick with a view of the whole countryside. Charles said he would like to live in that house one day. His father told him that if he worked very hard, one day he might do so.

In 1822, when Charles was ten, his father was transferred to London, the capital city of England. The Dickens family moved to a neighborhood called Camden Town. London was a new world for Charles. There were over 1.3 million people living in London at that time. That was two hundred thousand more people than just twenty years earlier. London was growing fast.

New inventions had led to an increase in factory work. People who once lived in the country now moved to the city for factory jobs. These jobs were often low-paying, and there were not enough of them for all the people coming to London. Many children had to take care of themselves while their parents worked. The streets were dirty and noisy. They were filled with people, as well as carts, horses, and pigs.

Hungry, barefoot children dressed in rags played in the streets and begged for money. School was a luxury only families with money could afford.

At the Dickenses' home in Camden Town, Charles slept in a cupboard —like a closet—over the main stairway. Charles's older sister, Fanny, was sent to the Royal Academy of Music to study singing. Charles no longer went to school at all. There wasn't enough money.

Charles's mother had plans to start a school of her own. She sent him out to advertise the new school, but the only people who came were people to whom his father owed money. They banged on the door while his father hid upstairs. Sometimes John Dickens sent Charles to the pawnshop on Hampstead Road. Charles was sent out with dishes, furniture, and even his beloved books. The family lived huddled in two empty rooms with no money to pay for coal for the fire. They had sold everything they owned to the pawnshop.

Even in this difficult time, Charles was growing to love

London. He liked to listen to people talk on the street. He learned their accents and gestures and the slang they used. Whenever he heard an interesting story about someone, he remembered it.

Then a friend of the family had an idea. Charles could earn money working at Warren' s blacking factory. For Charles this was terrible news. He felt as if his parents didn't think his life was worth anything.

At the blacking factory—at 30 Strand and then later on Chandos Street—Charles worked with two other boys, Bob Fagin and Poll Green. Charles was supposed to have lessons during his short dinner break. But the lessons didn't last long. He lived like every other factory boy, working ten hours a day, six days a week.

Bob and Poll sometimes called Charles the " young gentleman" because he spoke and behaved like someone who had been educated. In England at that time, it would have been very unusual for a poor boy like Bob Fagin to

Child Labor

The growth of factories and businesses in the nineteenth century meant many children were sent to work. Children as young as four years old had jobs. They worked up to sixteen hours a day in dangerous conditions. Sometimes they were beaten if they didn't work hard enough. Poor families depended on the money their children earned as trade apprentices, machine operators, household servants, and coal miners. Young children worked at factories making everything from blankets to matches to nails. The pay was as little as a half a penny per hour. By the early decades of the twentieth century, people were becoming outraged by the cruelties of child labor. Currently, almost every country in the world has laws aimed at preventing child labor.

ever advance into “polite” or high society. Charles was afraid that he would become a factory worker for life, just as Bob probably would be.

Charles’s small salary wasn’t enough to pay his father’s debts. On February 20, 1824, John Dickens was thrown into the Marshalsea Prison because of all the money he owed.

Chapter 2

Hidden Talents

The Marshalsea Prison was a debtors' prison. John Dickens had to stay there until he paid what he owed.

Except for Charles and Fanny, the whole family moved into Marshalsea Prison. Fanny boarded at her music school, and Charles moved in with Mrs. Roylance, a woman who rented rooms to working children. She didn't treat Charles very well. Every Sunday, Charles and Fanny would walk twelve miles to visit the family. On one of these visits, Charles convinced his father to find him a nicer place to stay, but he never forgot the terrible Mrs. Roylance.

His father's troubles had made Charles terrified of debt. When he got his own pay each week, he divided the coins

Marshalsea Prison

Marshalsea Prison in Southwark, London, was founded in the 1300s on the bank of the River Thames. It held people who had committed many different crimes, including accumulating large debts. Sometimes entire families were imprisoned, not just the parent who had committed a crime. If the prisoners had some money, they could buy things at the prison shops or restaurants and live in one of the nicer rooms. They could also buy a pass to leave the prison and earn the money to pay off their debts. Many prisoners racked up more debts while in prison, and the poorest people were crammed into the worst rooms. Many starved to death within months.

Marshalsea Prison was torn down in the 1870s. Only a single wall remains, where a plaque with a quote from Charles Dickens reads: "It is gone now, and the world is none the worse without it."

into seven equal piles. He wrapped those in little sacks and wrote the name of each day of the week on a different stack of coins. The sack for Wednesday would never be opened until that day. In this way, Charles learned to spend money only when necessary.

In May 1824, John Dickens was released from prison. He had inherited enough money to pay off his debts. Soon Charles no longer had to work at Warren's.

His mother was angry that Charles was no longer working. She wanted to send him back. To Charles, his father was a hero for rescuing him from the factory, and his mother was a villain. "I never afterwards forgot, I never shall forget, I never can forget, that my mother was warm for my being sent back," Charles said. The family never spoke of it again.

Charles returned to school. At Wellington House Academy, the teachers were strict, but Charles loved it. After so many months at the factory, he threw himself into games, theater, and jokes. He hid mice and bees in his desk, and made tiny stagecoaches for the mice to ride. He wrote stories and started his own newspaper. Other boys paid for copies with marbles. He made the boys laugh by pretending to speak in a foreign language he had made up himself.

Only two years later, when Charles was fifteen, his father fell into debt once again and could no longer pay for school. Charles went to work as a clerk at the Ellis and Blackmore law firm in May 1827. On his first day, he wore a military-style cap that tied under his chin. When his new bosses sent him out on an errand, he came back with a black eye!

Charles explained that a man in the street had made fun of his cap and knocked it off, and they had gotten into a fight. His bosses weren't shocked by the story, but they were shocked by how he told the story. He acted it out for them, playing both parts, plus the parts of onlookers. When he imitated the man making fun of his hat, his bosses couldn't stop laughing.

The more they spoke to their young clerk, the more amazed Ellis and Blackmore were by how well he knew London— the streets, the stories, the colorful characters. Their new clerk had hidden talents as a storyteller!

Chapter 3

Introducing Boz

Charles worked as a law clerk until 1829. When he was seventeen, he became a newspaper reporter in the law courts. Sometimes he wrote funny stories that pointed out the unfairness of the laws at that time. For Charles, the courts were another place to observe how people behaved and to hear interesting stories.

At this same time, Charles met a young woman named Maria Beadnell. She was the daughter of a banker. Charles fell madly in love with her. Some nights after leaving the court at two in the morning, he walked miles to stand in front of her house. He wrote letters to her parents. He said what a good match he was for their daughter, even though he didn't have much money.

Maria's family was not impressed. Her mother never even bothered to get Charles's name right. She referred to him as "Mr. Dickin." In 1832, Maria's parents sent her away to Paris.

With Maria gone, Charles focused on his writing. By the end of 1833, Charles had written a funny story about two cousins having dinner. He dropped the story, called "Dinner at Poplar Walk" into a "dark letter-box, in a dark office, up a dark court in Fleet Street." This was the office of the *Monthly Magazine*. A few days later, Charles bought a copy of the magazine and found the story printed there!

Charles's name didn't appear with the story. He didn't even get paid for it, but *Monthly Magazine* wanted more stories from the young writer. Instead of signing himself "Charles Dickens" in the magazine, he used the name "Boz." He borrowed the name from his youngest brother, Augustus, who was nicknamed Moses. As a toddler, Augustus pronounced it as “Boses,” which became “Boz” for short.

Charles wanted to write a longer story about a group of friends who form a club. *The Pickwick Papers*, his first novel, wasn’t published as a book at first. Instead, it appeared one chapter a month, starting in March 1836. People loved Charles’s characters, especially the servant Sam Weller. Charles wrote Weller’s words with a Cockney accent, the very way he had heard people speak on the streets of London: “Werry sorry to ’casion any personal inconvenience, ma’am, as the house-breaker said to the old lady when he put her on the fire . . .”

Everyone was talking about *The Pickwick Papers* and Boz. No one knew that Charles Dickens was the real author of the novel. But that would soon change.

Now that Charles was becoming successful, he felt it was time to get married. There wasn’t anyone he loved the way he had Maria Beadnell, but in the winter of 1836 he had met Catherine Hogarth through her father, a newspaper editor. If Charles wasn't exactly in love with Catherine, he did *like* her an awful lot, and he was very good friends with her younger sister, Mary. On April 2, 1836, Catherine and Charles were married. A month later they were expecting their first child.

Serialized Books

In the nineteenth century, many books were written one chapter at a time. A single chapter would be published in a magazine each month. A magazine was usually thirty-two pages and came wrapped in green paper. People would buy each issue of the magazine to read the next part of the story. This was good for publishers, because it made people eager to buy magazines. For people who didn't have much money, a few pennies a month was an affordable way to read a novel.

Once the whole story was complete, the publisher would sell a bound book. Those who could afford it bought the story as a book.

Charles Dickens had contracts with more than one publisher. Each contract was an agreement that Charles would write a book in installments for that publisher. His first novel, *The Pickwick Papers*, was published by Chapman and Hall. *Oliver Twist*, which he wrote at the same time, was published in the magazine *Bentley's Miscellany* and published by Richard Bentley.

Chapter 4

A Whole New World

Charles and Catherine moved to the Holborn neighborhood of London with Catherine's sister Mary.

Even though he hadn't yet finished *The Pickwick Papers*, Charles signed a contract to start a new novel. *Oliver Twist* is the story of an orphan boy who is kicked out of a workhouse for asking for more food. He runs away to London and falls in with a gang of thieves. The gang's leaders are the Artful Dodger and the villainous Fagin, who was named after Charles's old friend at the blacking factory.

Charles wrote both novels at once, scribbling madly with his quill pen. Every month he wrote one chapter for each book. The two books were very different. When the hero of *The Pickwick Papers* was having funny adventures, Oliver Twist was running for his life.

In addition to writing for *Monthly Magazine*, Charles quit court reporting and became the editor of a newspaper, *Bentley's Miscellany*. He chose stories, made sure they were printed correctly, and helped other writers. Most people would consider any *one* of these jobs—writing a novel, writing a second novel, or editing *Bentley's*—to be full-time work. Charles did all three at once and was also writing a play at the same time!

Charles's son, Charley, was born in January 1837. Charles called his new son "the infant phenomenon." He wrote the scene of Oliver Twist's birth just a few weeks after Charley was born and probably used his own son for inspiration.

Life at home was happy. Then, on May 7, 1837, Charles heard a scream from his sister-in-law Mary's room. She was very sick. She had been perfectly well just minutes before, and she was only seventeen. Yet the next afternoon, Mary

The Workhouse

A workhouse was a place where the poor in England could work in exchange for their food and housing. Because many of the workhouse residents had no skills, they often had to do difficult, but boring, work like breaking stones and unraveling old ropes so that the fibers could be reused. Life in a workhouse was not pleasant, but it was better than living on the street. Children in workhouses received some education and medical care, which they wouldn't have gotten outside the workhouse. It was not until the passing of the National Assistance Act of 1948 that the last workhouse in England was closed.

died in Charles's arms. Doctors thought it might have been her heart.

That month there were no new chapters of *The Pickwick Papers* or *Oliver Twist*. Charles was too heartbroken to write. It was the only time in his career he ever missed a deadline.

After Mary's death, Charles and Catherine took a vacation away from London. Charles spent a lot of time with a new friend, John Forster, a literary editor. It was a friendship that would last the rest of his life.

Charles's next books, including *Nicholas Nickleby* and *Barnaby Rudge*, were all published under his real name. His book *The Old Curiosity Shop* became so popular in America that when ships arrived with the magazines that contained a new chapter, people shouted from the docks for news about its young heroine: "Does Little Nell still live?" Charles thought a lot about visiting America. He often received fan mail from his American readers.

On January 2, 1842, Charles and Catherine traveled by

steamship to the United States. They left their children—Charley and two daughters, Mamie and Katey—behind in England.

There were many things Charles didn' t like about America. American publishers had been making money off his books without paying him! When Charles complained, reporters published stories about him that were not very kind. Crowds of American fans followed him everywhere. Newspapers said that Charles had " more animation than grace and more intelligence than beauty." Charles was used to being the person who described other people. He was not used to reading about himself!

Charles and Catherine returned to England on June 29, 1842. Another of Catherine's sisters, Georgina, came to live with them. Charles was happy to be away from America, a country he described as "driven by a herd of rascals."

Chapter 5

Scrooges and Micawbers

In December 1843, Charles finished a story about a mean old man visited by three ghosts on Christmas Eve. *A Christmas Carol* was published as a small book bound in red cloth with gold edging on its pages. It sold six thousand copies in just five days!

A Christmas Carol was a sensation.

In January, the Dickenses welcomed another son, Francis. Charles and Catherine now had five children.

Charles's daughter Mamie once said her father wrote furiously at his desk, then jumped up and went to the mirror. He made all sorts of faces, then ran back to write more. Again and again he returned to the mirror, acting out scenes and talking out loud. He didn't even see Mamie there. He had completely become the characters he was hard at work creating.

Those characters had finally brought Charles the security he longed for as a child. Now that Charles had money, he wanted to use it to help others.

None of Charles's new friends knew about his family's past, except John Forster. John was the only person Charles ever told about it, but in 1849, Charles started work on *David Copperfield*. This book borrowed many details from real life—Charles's father's spending, the debtors' prison, leaving school for the factory, his mean landlady—and turned them into a best seller. So many people read *David Copperfield* that the book began to influence the way people spoke. A man who was always in debt but cheerfully expected that money would come from somewhere became known as a "Micawber" after a character in the book. Charles's friends all recognized that "Micawber" was John Dickens, but they

A Christmas Carol

A Christmas Carol not only changed the way people thought about Charles Dickens, it changed the way people thought about Christmas. Some historians believe that many of our holiday traditions, such as parties, family gatherings, Christmas feasts, dancing, and games, were inspired by the book. The name "Scrooge" came to refer to any stingy, unkind person, just as "Bah, humbug!" came to mean "That's nonsense!" Even the phrase "Merry Christmas!" was made popular by the book. A few months after its publication, there was a surge of money given to charities in Britain. People were inspired to be generous! In America, a factory owner was so moved by the story that he gave all his workers Christmas Day off and gave each one of them a turkey!

still never suspected that he had ever been in debtors' prison.

At the end of that year, Charles, who had left his job at *Bentley's Miscellany* some years earlier, decided to start his own monthly magazine called *Household Words*. It contained stories by Charles and his friends William Thackeray and Wilkie Collins.

In August 1850, Catherine had her ninth child, Dora Annie Dickens. It wasn't easy for Catherine to be pregnant so often. Her sister Georgina often took care of the children. Catherine didn't see Charles much because he was always working. She couldn't even take a walk with him because he walked too fast. He said his inspiration came from the crowded streets. He sometimes walked for thirty miles at a time! The more tired Catherine became, the more energy Charles seemed to have.

In 1851, when Dora was still a baby, John Dickens died from complications of an operation on his gallbladder. No matter how much trouble his father had caused him, Charles

Urania Cottage

In May 1846, Charles, along with an heiress named Angela Burdett-Coutts, founded a home for homeless women. Charles didn't want the women blamed for their problems. He wanted to educate them and provide training for household skills. He wanted to give them hope.

More than one hundred women graduated from Urania Cottage between 1847 and 1859.

WILKIE COLLINS (1824-1889)

William Wilkie Collins was a novelist, playwright, and close friend of Charles Dickens. His most famous novels include *The Woman in White* and *The Moonstone*, the first detective novel in the English language. *The Moonstone* was his most popular novel and paved the way for other fictional detective stories such as *The Sherlock Holmes Mysteries*. He said of his early days with Dickens, "We saw each other every day, and were as fond of each other as men could be."

forgave him and paid off every one of his debts.

Two weeks after his father's death, baby Dora suddenly died. Charles was heartbroken, but—as always—he kept working.

Chapter 6

Back to Gad's Hill

Between Charles's new book, *Bleak House, Household Words*, and Urania Cottage, he had little time to relax. When he had a kidney infection, he took only six days off work.

Catherine had had her tenth and last child, Edward, in 1852. In his letters to friends, Charles started to mention trouble at home. He and Catherine were growing apart, but Charles never said why. In Charles's next novel, *Hard Times*, the hero was married to a woman who wasn't right for him, but the law wouldn't let him divorce her. Many thought this was a reflection of the Dickenses' own marriage.

Charley Dickens, now eighteen, was at school at Eton. Charles planned to send his second son, Walter, to India to work for a British company. To others, Charles's family looked perfect—like the families in the stories he often wrote about in his magazine.

In February 1855, on a visit to Chatham, Charles saw that the house he had liked so much on Gad's Hill was for sale. Charles decided to buy it. He had worked hard for many years, and now he was going to live in the very house he had once admired.

In November of that same year, Charles and Wilkie Collins were writing a play together called *The Frozen Deep*. It was based on the Franklin expedition, a group of English explorers who had gotten lost in the Arctic ten years earlier in 1845. Their frozen bodies had recently been discovered.

The play was about the explorers' last days. Charles played the starring role of the expedition's leader, Richard Wardour. He was also the play's director and stage manager.

The Frozen Deep was a big success in England. People loved how Charles played the doomed Richard Wardour.

Charles's daughters Mamie and Katey had parts in the show, as did his sister-in-law Georgina. They even gave a private performance for Queen Victoria.

In August 1857, not long after sixteen-year-old Walter Dickens left for India, Charles was invited to perform *The Frozen Deep* at the Free Trade Hall. It was a big theater. Charles would need professional actresses to put the show on in that large a space. A friend recommended Frances Ternan and her three daughters, Fanny, Maria, and Ellen, who was known as Nelly.

Queen Victoria (1819-1901)

Queen Victoria was the ruling monarch of the United Kingdom of Great Britain and Ireland from June 1837 until her death in 1901. She helped maintain peace and prosperity in her country, and she ruled during a time in which exciting new discoveries were made in many fields, including science, industry, engineering, recreation, and medicine.

The span of her reign is so important that the nineteenth century in England is known as the Victorian Era. Many great English novels were written at this time, including *Alice's Adventures in Wonderland* and *Jane Eyre*, as well as the *Adventures of Sherlock Holmes stories*.

Chapter 7

The Worst of Times

Nelly Ternan was only eighteen years old when she met Charles. His friends knew that he loved her dearly, but publicly Charles said they were just friends. Catherine never spoke badly of Charles. She accepted his wish that they now live mostly apart.

By 1858, Charles lived at Gad's Hill with his children and their aunt Georgina. Catherine lived in London with a housekeeper. Laws at the time made divorce so expensive that hardly anyone could afford to do it. They agreed to lead separate lives instead.

Charles's life was busier than ever. When a friend of his died, Charles wanted to raise money for his family. He wrote a new version of *A Christmas Carol* to read for an audience. He played all the characters, using different voices. The audience loved it. Charles, too, loved the performances—and the money they brought in. He went on a three-month tour in England, Scotland, and Ireland reading his work.

There was a lot of gossip about the Dickenses' marriage. This made Charles furious.

If Charles's friends stood up for Catherine, Charles no longer considered them friends! He even fought about it with the other workers at *Household Words*. In January 1859, he announced he was shutting down the magazine. He even stopped working on behalf of Urania Cottage.

Charles's friends were horrified at how he was acting and so were his children. He now claimed that they had never loved Catherine and she never loved them. When the children spoke to their mother, he got angry at them. His daughter Katey later said that her father "behaved like a madman."

The house on Gad's Hill had become a terrible, sad

place. Katey escaped by marrying Wilkie Collins's sickly brother, Charles, an artist, in July 1860. On Katey's wedding day, Mamie found her father holding Katey's wedding dress and crying. He blamed himself for driving her away from home. Catherine wasn't even invited to the wedding.

Charles put his energy into a new magazine, *All the Year Round*. Charles decided to publish his next novel as a serial in its pages. It was about the French Revolution. Charles had a rough time getting started on the story. In time, the opening of *A Tale of Two Cities* became one of the most famous first lines of any book ever written: "It was the best of times, it was the worst of times."

Chapter 8

New Journeys

In the neighborhood of Gad's Hill there was a cemetery. One family had thirteen gravestones marking thirteen children who had died. It gave Charles an idea for a story called *Great Expectations*. It would be published in *All the Year Round* after *A Tale of Two Cities*. The story begins in a graveyard. A poor young orphan, Pip, runs into an escaped convict there. Years later, Pip is given the chance to become a gentleman and join polite society.

After *Great Expectations*, Charles went on more reading tours. With so many broken relationships in his life, he took great comfort from audiences who loved him for his work. In September 1863, his mother died, but Charles didn't feel the kind of forgiveness for her that he'd felt for his father. He always remembered that it was his mother who wanted him to return to his job at Warren's. Two months later, in December 1863, Charles's son Walter died in India.

In June 1865, Charles, Nelly, and Nelly's mother were on a train to London. While crossing a bridge in Kent, the train jumped the tracks. It broke in two parts. Charles and the Ternans were thrown into one corner of a train car that hung halfway off the bridge. Charles later described the scene to a friend: "No imagination can conceive the ruin of the carriages, or the extraordinary weights under which the people were lying, or the complications into which they were twisted up among iron and wood, and mud and water."

Charles climbed out through the window and got the Ternans to a waiting ambulance train. He went back to help others trapped in the wreckage. He sat with the injured and the dying. Then he climbed back into his own carriage to retrieve the book he had been working on: *Our Mutual*

Friend.

The following year, Charles planned a special tour to the United States.

Charles's second visit to America in 1867 was better than his first visit back in 1842. Crowds loved his readings. He saw old friends. Instead of facing questions about his book sales, he was performing for fans who welcomed him and cheered for his characters.

Charles's health was not the best. His foot was sometimes so swollen he couldn't walk, and he had trouble eating. Yet he traveled from Boston to New York to Philadelphia to Washington, DC. President Andrew Johnson even attended a reading and invited him to the White House.

Charles didn't regret returning to the United States one bit. On the boat home, in May 1868, he was already planning another reading tour.

Kate Wiggin (1856-1923)

On a train from Maine to Boston, a twelve-year-old girl from Philadelphia slipped into the seat beside the great author Charles Dickens. She'd read all his books several times, but "of course [she did] skip some of the very dull parts once in a while; not the short dull parts, but the long ones." They talked about which parts were dull and which books were their favorites—they both loved *David Copperfield* best. Kate Wiggin never forgot her wonderful trip with her favorite author, even after she grew up to become a best-selling author herself. Kate Wiggin published *Rebecca of Sunnybrook Farm* in 1903.

Chapter 9

Terror to the End

Some might have expected Charles Dickens to spend the summer of 1868 resting after his trip. Instead, he was planning a new, secret performance that would surprise all his friends.

At the end of the summer, his son Henry left for Trinity Hall at Cambridge University to study mathematics. Edward was going to join his brother Alfred farming in Australia.

Charles started his reading tour in October. In November, Charley became an editor at *All the Year Round*.

That same month, Charles unveiled the secret scene he was planning to perform. In *Oliver Twist*, a criminal named Bill Sykes catches his girlfriend, Nancy, trying to help the orphan, Oliver. In a fit of rage, he kills her. Terrified of what he's done, he runs away and is later killed by the police. Charles was going to perform it all onstage.

The scene was exciting and terrifying. Charles threw himself into the part of the evil Bill Sykes, whipping himself into a frenzy that was almost too real for his audience. In his own copy of the scene, Charles made a note to himself: "Terror to the End." That's exactly what he gave audiences.

When it was finished, he was so exhausted he had to be helped offstage. But once he felt better, he wanted to do it again. Like any great actor, he loved the power he had over the audience.

His doctor ordered him to quit the tour completely, but Charles refused. The doctor told Charley Dickens to go to every performance. If his father seemed like he was going to fall down, the doctor had told him, "You must run up there and catch him . . . or, by Heaven, he'll die before them all!" In April 1869, Charles took a break from the tour, but he wouldn't quit completely.

While resting, Charles signed a contract with Chapman and Hall for a new book to be written in twelve parts: *The Mystery of Edwin Drood*.

For the illustrations in this new book, Charles hoped to hire his son-in-law, Charles Collins. Katey's husband needed the money, but he was too sick to do the work. Charles had never liked Katey marrying someone so unwell. He later said that Charles Collins had just "collapsed for the whole term of his natural life." For someone as active as Charles Dickens, Charles Collins must have been difficult to understand.

Charles's foot was still painful, and one of his arms was numb. He had probably had a stroke, but ignored it. He couldn't come downstairs at Gad's Hill for most of Christmas 1869. One evening, he joined some of his family for traditional parlor games. In a memory game, everyone had to recite a list of items and add one more item for the next person. When they had been playing for a while, his son

The Dickens Children

All of Catherine and Charles's children were given special nicknames by their father. All lived very different lives:

Charles— Charley— Became an editor at *All Around the World*.

Mamie— Mild Glo'ster— Never married, lived with her Aunt Georgina after Charles's death.

Katey—Lucifer Box—Became a widow and then married an artist and became an artist herself.

Walter—Young Skull—Died young in India.

Francis—Chickenstalker—Joined the mounted police in Canada.

Alfred—Sampson Brass or Skittles—Became a farmer in Australia.

Sydney—The Ocean Spectre or The Admiral—Became an officer in the Royal Navy.

Henry—Mr. H—Became a very respected judge.

Edward—the Plornishghenter or Plorn—Went into politics in Australia.

Henry said, Charles "had successfully gone through the long string of words, and finished up with his own contribution: 'Warren's Blacking, 30 Strand!'"

Charles said it with a strange look in his eye, as if the words had special meaning for him. Henry didn't know what that meaning could be. Nearly fifty years later, Charles was still haunted by the shame of having worked in the blacking factory and still kept it a secret from almost everyone.

Chapter 10

Poet's Corner

Charles Dickens was no longer the boy in the window at Warren's blacking factory. He was the most popular writer in the world. He'd written over fifteen novels. He'd traveled all over Europe and North America. He'd been chased by adoring crowds. He'd appeared in front of theaters packed with fans. His books were translated into many languages. Even his least popular books sold well. He received letters from all over the world. He'd created words that had been added to the dictionary. Where once his family had been threatened with eviction from their home, he now owned more than one beautiful house, including the one he'd dreamed of living in as a child. Amazingly, he'd stayed popular for decades.

The first chapter of *Edwin Drood* appeared on March 31, 1870. It sold an amazing fifty thousand copies in its first few days of release. Thirty-four years after the publication of *The Pickwick Papers*, Charles Dickens was a sensation all over again. "As he delighted the fathers, so he delights the children," said the London *Times*.

Every morning at Gad's Hill, Charles wrote in a small Swiss chalet given to him by a friend who sent it in pieces from Switzerland. Charles loved writing in the upper story where the mirrors on the walls reflected the trees and the river outside.

On June 4, 1870, Katey came for a visit. They had a long talk. Katey was surprised by the kind of things her father said. He told her he wished he'd been a better father and a better man. He talked about his relationship with Nelly and the end of his marriage. He spoke, Katey later said, "as though his life was over and there was nothing left."

Katey left the next day. On June 8, Charles spent the

morning in the chalet, writing. It was unusual for Charles to work in the afternoon, but on this day, after lunch, he returned to finish chapter six of *Edwin Drood*.

That evening at dinner with his sister-in-law Georgina, Charles had a stroke. Katey and Mamie rushed home to see him. He died the following day without ever waking up. It was June 9, 1870. Charles Dickens was only fifty-eight years old.

Charles had planned to be buried near Rochester Cathedral, but his country would accept nothing less than Westminster Abbey. Westminster Abbey is the most famous church in England. Many of the greatest writers in English history are buried there in what is called Poet's Corner. When Charles died, the London *Times* wrote an editorial saying he should be buried in Poet's Corner. The Dean of Westminster agreed and offered to bury him there. It was a great honor—one Charles's family could not refuse.

Charles had earned his place among the greatest British

writers. He was buried in a small, private ceremony, but so many people came to bring flowers that the church had to keep the grave open for two days to hold all the crowds. People from all walks of life made their way to Westminster Abbey to say good-bye to him. There was no other person in England so beloved by people of all classes, rich and poor. To this day, a wreath is laid on his grave every year on his birthday.

The very next year, John Forster published a biography of his friend Charles Dickens. For the first time, people learned that Charles did not have the happy childhood that his readers assumed he had. They learned just how much David Copperfield *was* Charles Dickens. They saw that Charles had sympathy for people in all parts of society because he had been both poor and rich. The part of his life that he had always hidden—the poverty, hard work, and shame of prison—was the very thing that made his writing so special and so loved by so many.

Timeline of Charles Dickens's Life

1812	—	Charles Dickens born in Portsmouth.
1817	—	Dickens family moves to Chatham, England.
1822	—	Dickens family moves to London, England.
1824	—	Charles starts work in the blacking factory.
1825	—	Charles returns to school.
1833	—	"A Dinner at Poplar Walk" published in *Monthly Magazine.*
1836	—	Charles marries Catherine Hogarth.
1837	—	Catherine's sister Mary Hogarth dies.
1842	—	Charles visits the United States.
1843	—	*A Christmas Carol* is published.
1846	—	Urania Cottage is founded.
1850	—	First issue of *Household Words* is published.
1854	—	*Hard Times* is published.
1857	—	Charles separates from his wife.
1859	—	*A Tale of Two* Cities is published.
1865	—	Charles is in a train crash in Kent.
1867	—	Second tour of the United States.
1870	—	Charles Dickens dies.

Timeline of the World

About 970	Work on Westminster Abbey begins.
1450	Gutenberg printing press is invented in Germany.
1606	*Macbeth* is written by William Shakespeare.
1666	Great Fire of London destroys much of the city.
1749	*Tom Jones* by Henry Fielding is published.
1770	Ludwig van Beethoven is born.
1789	French Revolution begins.
1795	Napoleon Bonaparte invades the Netherlands.
1812	War of 1812 breaks out.
1825	Japan closes its ports to foreign ships.
1830	Poland revolts against Russian rule.
1837	Victoria is crowned queen of England.
1852	Devil's Island penal colony is opened.
1857	Hollywood is founded.
1865	First commercially sold typewriter is invented.

Bibliography

* Manning, Mick, and Brita Granström. Charles Dickens: Scenes from an Extraordinary Life. London: Frances Lincoln Children's Books, 2011.

Slater, Michael. Charles Dickens. New Haven, CT: Yale University Press, 2009.

Smiley, Jane. Charles Dickens: A Life. New York: Penguin, 2002.

* Stanley, Diane, and Peter Vennema. Charles Dickens: The Man Who Had Great Expectations. New York: Morrow Junior Books, 1993.

Tomalin, Claire. Charles Dickens: A Life. New York: Penguin, 2011.

* Warren, Andrea. Charles Dickens and the Street Children of London. New York: Houghton Mifflin Books for Children, 2011.

* Books for young readers